How Many Women Does It Take to Change a Redneck?

Jeff Foxworthy

With illustrations by David Boyd

Rutledge Hill Press®

Nashville, Tennessee

A Division of Thomas Nelson Publishers

www.thomasnelson.com

Published by Rutledge Hill Press, a Division of Thomas Nelson, Inc., P.O. Box 141000, Nashville, Tennessee 37214.

Rutledge Hill Press books may be purchased in bulk for educational, business, fundraising, or sales promotional use. For information, please e-mail SpecialMarkets@ThomasNelson.com.

Library of Congress Cataloging-in-Publication Data

Foxworthy, Jeff.
    How many women does it take to change a redneck? / Jeff Foxworthy ; with illustrations by David Boyd.
        p. cm.
    ISBN-13: 978-1-4016-0329-8 (pbk.)
    ISBN-10: 1-4016-0329-7 (pbk.)
    1. Rednecks—Humor. I. Boyd, David. II. Title.
PN6231.R38F6735 2006
818'.5402—dc22   2006022408

Printed in the United States of America

05 06 07 08 09 — 5 4 3 2 1

Contents

Introduction

How many women does it take to change a redneck?

Not since the first redneck tried to figure out second cousins has there been a more perplexing question. And like the answer to most of life's puzzles, the answer to this one is, "Depends."

Depends on why you'd want to change a redneck in the first place. A true redneck is like a piece of original art—colorful and exciting. When the color gets outside the lines, there's no need to tear up the page and start over. That just makes the art more interesting. And when the excitement gets outside the lines, it's always interesting . . . such as who drove into a tree, who fell out of a window, and who spent a night in jail.

Depends on whether it's actually possible to change a redneck. As a general rule, rednecks are born into that glorious state. Like father, like son. So trying to change a redneck is like trying to teach a frog to sing—it frustrates the frog and irritates the devil out of the teacher. Or, as my grandmother used to say, "No horse's ass ever stopped being one just because you told him he was."

Depends on whether the redneck wants to change. There are times when a redneck might be willing to alter his behavior without pressure from women. For example, he might change out of

his work clothes and into something more appropriate if Paris Hilton was dropping by after work. Then again, he wouldn't even change his socks if it was his mother-in-law dropping by.

Depends on how long he'd have to change. In certain circumstances, such as being on the wrong end of a shotgun or an iron skillet, rednecks can make immediate and dramatic changes. But those changes tend to last about as long as a cold beer or repentance. Vows to change that are accompanied by sexual activity usually last until daybreak.

Throughout this book, I'll give you a few more answers to that great philosophical question, "How many women does it take to change a redneck?" In between, I'll provide lots of tips on how a redneck should conduct himself so that no woman or her mother would ever consider asking him to change. And, of course, I'll give you plenty of ways to determine if "You Might Be a Redneck . . ."

That's sort of like killing three birds with one electrified clothesline.

First Impressions

The first thing you notice about a redneck is his appearance . . . unless he's been hunting for three days, in which case the scent will often arrive first. So that's where I'll begin my advice.

Most rednecks grew up with their mamas holding them down in a bathtub twice a week and scrubbing away like they were digging for potatoes. That was enough to turn anybody against baths. Then, as rednecks got a little older and were allowed to bathe themselves, they figured out the contradiction of tub bathing: why would anybody wash their face with water they were sitting in? That revelation also didn't encourage regular bathing.

Shortly afterward, most rednecks started being interested in girls outside their own family, but they quickly realized that girls were not interested in them if they smelled like a mop bucket. More times than not, some degree of personal grooming was going to be required for rednecks to become socially active. Rather than have mamas bathing their grown sons twice a week, I came up with these tips for modern redneck men who may seek the company of others.

1

Bathing—How Much, How Often

It has been scientifically proven that regular bathing goes a long way toward a lice-free lifestyle, and soap is one of the fundamental tools of bathing. Some rednecks depend on the old reliable—lye soap. Others think lye is harsh on the skin, so they make their own soap out of rendered animal fat scented with Gummi Bears. Store-bought soap is also available for those seeking to improve their stations in life. My personal favorite is the NASCAR series, where the bars of soap are shaped and colored like miniature racecars.

I recommend bathing at home, instead of taking a bar of soap to the local YMCA or the public pool. Cleaning the ring out of a swimming pool can take forever and may delay your spouse from starting her normal household chores.

A garden hose set on "spray" or "mist" and hung over a tree branch makes an ideal shower. Have your sister hold up a sheet so the sight of you bathing doesn't scare the chickens.

Many modern subdivisions and trailer parks have man-made ponds or lakes on the property. These provide an excellent opportunity for bathing *au naturel*, which means "naked outdoors." The only dangers associated with outdoor naked bathing are leeches, broken beer bottles, water moccasins, rusty nails, and jealous, heavily armed husbands, but the unfettered joy of outdoor naked bathing more than makes up for the risks. There is one other important thing to remember, however: friends don't let friends bathe drunk. So if your friend is drunk and insists on bathing *au naturel*, leave before he takes off his clothes.

Finally, the misfortune of a leaking roof can be turned into a trendy shower with careful planning and a washtub. If the leak happens to be between your favorite recliner and the TV when your wife wants to shower, a funnel and hose can be used to redirect the flow out of your field of vision. On the other hand, if your wife's good-looking sister is visiting and wants to shower, the funnel and hose can be used to bring her back into your view. It's sort of like hitting the "channel recall" button on the remote late on a Saturday night—auto racing, naked woman, auto racing, naked woman . . .

3

You've ever been third through
the bath water.

You Might Be a Redneck If . . .

You don't meet the hygiene
standards at a water park.

☆

You have to wash your hands *before*
you go to the bathroom.

☆

You offer somebody the shirt off your back
. . . and they won't take it.

☆

Your idea of conservation is moving your
Saturday-night bath to every other Saturday night.

☆

Chiggers are included on your list
of top five hygiene problems.

You made a homemade hot tub
with a trolling motor.

You own all the components
of soap-on-a-rope except the soap.

☆

You have a hook in your shower to hang your hat on.

Shaving

Electric razors are a modern inconvenience that I do not recommend. In the first place, electricity is not always available. And secondly, even if your razor is battery operated, swapping the batteries back and forth from your razor to your flashlight could leave you without an emergency light on the roadside some dark night. You can't flag down help with a buzzing razor.

The first rule of shaving is to take your time. A few days' contemplation is recommended. A man who is always clean shaven runs the risk of being labeled a sissy or a banker.

When the time comes, start by lathering your beard with soapsuds or your kids' bubble bath. If you use commercial shaving cream, avoid anything that is scented with flowers or fruit (see earlier note about sissies and bankers). Drag your razor lightly over the area to be shaved with just enough pressure to remove the suds but not enough to remove all facial hair. Remember, the point of shaving is to look like you haven't for two days. When you've finished the process, rinse the razor and return it to your tackle box.

If you cut yourself while shaving, simply apply a small piece of toilet paper to the wound. It is best to remove the toilet paper before you arrive at work, although some women find it particularly alluring. If the bleeding has not stopped within twenty-four hours, a stitch or two may be required. (*Warning:* Never apply a tourniquet to the neck.)

You use the shaving cream made
for tough beards . . . and so does your wife.

☆

People can tell what you had for breakfast
by looking at your beard.

☆

Your girlfriend ever had to shave her legs
to get a pair of pants to fit.

Your wife
has ever
burned
out your
electric
razor.

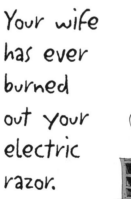

Ears

While ears need to be cleaned regularly, this is a job that should be done in private using one's own truck keys. (*Note*: Keys also must be cleaned regularly, because earwax buildup can short-circuit a starter switch.) Post office box keys are recommended for deep-ear probing. Remember to stop pushing when you encounter resistance.

For serious wax buildup, do not rule out a garden hose as a hygiene partner.

- A recent innovation in cleaning out ears is ear wicks, or candles. You insert one of these specially designed candles in your ear and light it. The draft from the burning candle draws wax out of the ear and into the candle cone. Although this technique seems to work well, it is not without risks.

- Light the candle before sticking it in your ear. Otherwise, your favorite cap could go up in flames.

- Do not use birthday candles, especially those in the shape of numbers. The five is almost impossible to fit into the average ear.

Do not mix earwax with candle wax, unless you want your candles to grow ear hair.

Tending to ear hair should be considered a normal part of ear maintenance. Ear hair is most attractive when combed into the sideburns, or, if you feel particularly adventurous, it can be combed behind the ear for a startling effect. For side-sleepers, remember that bed-head can impact ear hair the same way it does scalp hair.

Hair Care

Contrary to popular belief, dandruff is not an incurable disease. And despite what the guys around the gas pump say, shampooing regularly is not the leading cause of sissiness (although kiwi-scented shampoo will make you want to be a waiter). Some women, in fact, actually find clean

hair virile and attractive. For best results, brush hair before it dries completely or else pull a stocking cap down low over your head while the hair dries. (*Warning*: Do not visit your bank while wearing the stocking cap, unless you've got nothing planned for the next five to seven years.)

If you can afford store-bought hair tonic, use it. But don't waste your money on anything labeled "the dry look," because the same effect can be achieved by driving around with your truck windows open.

If you're on a tight hygiene budget, many household items work just as well. Brake fluid, for example, not only holds the hair in place but adds a dark, Elvis-like sheen to the scalp. Butter is especially effective on lighter colored hair and creates the illusion of highlights; for those with cholesterol issues, margarine is an acceptable alternative.

This may come as a great surprise to most rednecks, but mullets are out. On the positive side, as hairlines rise above the collar, it's easier to show off your masculine back hair with low-cut tank tops. Ironically enough, the Don Johnson *Miami Vice* look is back in, especially the beard stubble (see earlier tips on shaving). Once the hairs begin to curl, however, it's no longer considered stubble.

One thing that never changes is sideburns, where bigger is always better. The most popular style remains the pork-chop, where the bottom of the sideburn flares out to the edges of the mouth. Some creative rednecks prefer the gnawed spare-rib look, which is much thinner like its namesake.

You Might Be a Redneck If . . .

You forego a haircut because there's not a clean bowl in the house.

☆

You grow your sideburns longer and fuller because it looks so good on your sister.

☆

Both you and your wife wore ponytails for your wedding.

☆

You asked a hairstylist for a "business at the front, party at the back" cut.

You Might Be a Redneck If . . .

You get an estimate from the barber before he cuts your hair.

You Might Be a Redneck If . . .

Everyone in your family has the same haircut.

☆

You've never had a haircut from a nonrelative.

☆

You get your oil changed by your barber.

☆

People often mistake you for an Elvis impersonator.

☆

You've ever passed an afternoon watching
other people get their hair cut.

☆

Your hair stylist also cuts your grass.

Hair Color

Blond with black roots has always been a popular color for rednecks, but some retro trendsetters have recently gone to black with blond roots. This effect can be achieved by squirting peroxide directly onto the scalp area with the use of a syringe.

Some rednecks have been known to apply lemon juice to their hair to create highlights. Lemonade is an acceptable alternative for the younger generation, and "hard" lemonade is an option for those over 21.

Red spikes with black roots is another popular option, although the spikes require that you wear a cowboy hat instead of the usual baseball cap.

As rednecks grow older and gray starts creeping into their hair palette, many find that black liquid shoe polish combed into the hair daily maintains that youthful appearance.

Eyebrows

When eyebrows reach the length where they obscure your vision, it's time to mow. Growing them long and combing them backwards to cover a receding hairline is not considered fashionable. Thick eyebrows, however, do form a perfect resting place for reading glasses when not in use. For a rakish look, you can apply a little earwax to full eyebrows and curl the ends up, sort of like a handlebar moustache for the brow.

Your family trait is a uni-brow.

☆

Your wife touches up her eyebrows
with waterproof marker.

☆

You dye your hair and clean your floors
with the same stuff.

☆

Your favorite hair product is Clorox.

☆

You think "going back to your roots"
means growing out the peroxide.

You Might Be a Redneck If . . .

You've ever plucked a nose hair
with a pair of pliers.

☆

You can drink beer through your nose.

You've ever
been to an
eye, nose,
and throat
specialist to
have a finger
removed.

Nose Hair

Plucking these unwanted devils one at a time will work, but a cigarette lighter and a small tolerance for pain can accomplish the same goal and save hours. When using this method, keep a bucket of water nearby.

Dental Care

Scientists have proven that the use of a toothbrush (and toothpaste, when available) can help people keep their teeth well into their thirties and even beyond. Many people brush on a daily basis. Each and every tooth should be brushed, no matter how far apart they are. Your grandparents probably told you that they used baking soda or certain tree sap instead of toothpaste, but keep in mind that they probably delivered this wisdom through false teeth.

Unlike clothes and shoes, a toothbrush should never be a hand-me-down item.

You Might Be a Redneck If . . .

Your teeth are visible in your silhouette.

The dentist in your town went bankrupt.

All of your dental visits are emergencies.

Your dentist wanted to exhibit
your eyeteeth at a convention.

You Might Be a Redneck If . . .

You have to take the entire day off work
to get your teeth cleaned.

☆

Most days start with someone
in your house asking,
"Has anybody seen my teeth?"

You think
Old Yeller
is a movie
about your
brother's tooth.

Your dentist dreads seeing you more
than you dread seeing him.

☆

Your dentist has described you
as "the worst-case scenario."

☆

You choose your teeth from a catalog.

You tell Grandpa
he has something
in his teeth, and
he takes them
out to see.

24

You Might Be a Redneck If . . .

You've ever used duct tape
to repair dental work.

Your two-year-old has more teeth
than you do.

You've ever fixed your false teeth
with a glue gun.

☆

Your dentist has adult magazines
in his waiting room.

Flossing

Dental floss is the modern equivalent of broom straw. It can be purchased in most urban grocery stores or drugstores, but any loose thread on your clothing will work just as well and will tidy your appearance simultaneously. A lightweight monofilament fishing line also works wonderfully well. I recommend removing all lures from the line before flossing.

Manicures and Pedicures

Sometimes you may find it impossible to chew a fingernail evenly. Don't panic: household scissors or a sharp steak knife can usually handle the task. Toenails, however, present a tougher problem, and you may have to resort to a strong wood file or bolt-cutters to achieve the desired effect. Remember to always put nail clippings in their proper place—the ashtray.

Dirt and grease under nails is a social no-no, as they tend to detract from the taste of finger foods, unless you're having fried food or buffalo wings. A good pocketknife will take care of this problem and allow you to trim your cuticles at the same time. (*Note*: Cuticles are the skin around your nails, not the cute twins down the street.)

Most of the socks you own allow you
to cut some of your toenails while wearing them.

☆

You cut your toenails in front of company.

☆

You've ever used a toenail as a bookmark.

☆

You clean your hands daily with gasoline.

☆

Your toenail clippers say Craftsman on the side.

You Might Be a Redneck If . . .

You've ever injured a relative with a flying toenail.

☆

You set your shoes outside and the flowers died.

☆

You clean your fingernails with a stick.

☆

Your pocketknife doubles as a nail clipper
and a cheese slicer.

☆

You've tightened a loose screw
with your fingernail.

☆

You get Odor-Eaters as a Christmas present.

Corns and Calluses

Foot surgery is a budget buster, but expensive doctor visits can often be avoided by doing certain procedures in the privacy of one's own home or automobile. For example, corns and calluses can be removed using a common potato peeler. Remember never to cut against the grain.

Brightly colored tissue folded between toes with corns can provide moderate relief. Be sure to match the color of the tissue to your flip-flops or baseball cap. If a corn or bunion on the outside of your foot causes you to cut a relief hole in your shoe, remember to save the piece so it can be glued in later.

If your feet become cracked and callused in the summertime from walking barefooted around the yard, you can soften them up with a nightly application of lard. And as an added bonus, your feet will literally slide into your socks the next morning.

Deodorant, Perfume, Cologne, and Such

Proper use of these toiletries can forestall bathing for several days. If the problem has escalated to the point that you are applying them directly to your clothing instead of to your skin, a bath is inevitable.

Certain scents attract bees, so be leery of anything with "honey" in the name. On the other hand, you may want to encourage your girlfriend or wife to wear a scent that attracts deer and wild turkey; this can provide an opportunity for the two of you to spend time together during hunting season, and you can use her for bait.

If you live alone, deodorant is a waste of good money.

Your favorite cologne
is Deep Woods OFF!

Any dog can follow your scent.

☆

Your wife uses the air freshener
in your truck as deodorant.

☆

You have a prescription for antiperspirant.

Your wife thinks
toilet water is
exactly that.

HOW MANY WOMEN DOES IT TAKE TO CHANGE A REDNECK?

- ○ **MORE THAN IT TAKES TO CHANGE A TIRE.**

- ○ **TWELVE . . . IN A JURY BOX.**

ONLY ONE, IF HER AIM IS GOOD.

Fashion

Redneck fashion, like so many things red, is influenced by a desire to stand out in a crowd. Anybody can wear a pair of jeans, but by cutting holes in different places, drawing on them with different colored markers, and

walking off the hems to different lengths, each redneck can make a distinctive fashion statement. Similarly, many rednecks wear unbuttoned dress shirts, but they personalize the look with a custom belt buckle.

Although there's plenty of room for personal expression, the well-dressed redneck should follow some basic guidelines. Your choice of clothing can be summarized by three rules:

- "No collar, no tie." If you see a redneck wearing a tie, odds are 99–1 that he's dead and stretched out in a coffin.

- "Just say no to crack." Although plumbers are required by union regulations to show at least two inches of butt crack at all times, others are advised to save the show for home.

- "No shirt, no shoes, we're eating at home." After a long day on the job, nothing is more relaxing than taking off your shirt and shoes and bellying up to the table. Also, eating shirtless means fewer stains on your favorite work shirt.

Beyond those three guidelines, there is plenty of room for personalization.

The Redneck at Leisure

Past-dated T-bone, marked down for quick sale

Cold beer (nothing "lite" about it)

Six-pack stomach, redneck style

"Good" cap—just like his work cap, except cleaner

Thirty-fourth cigarette of the day

Grate custom-made with chicken wire

Woven vinyl beach chair, rescued from neighbor's garbage

Boxers that double as shorts/swim trunks

Grill purchased at yard sale for $2

No shirt, no shoes, no problem!

Best friend—they share a work ethic

The Redneck at Work

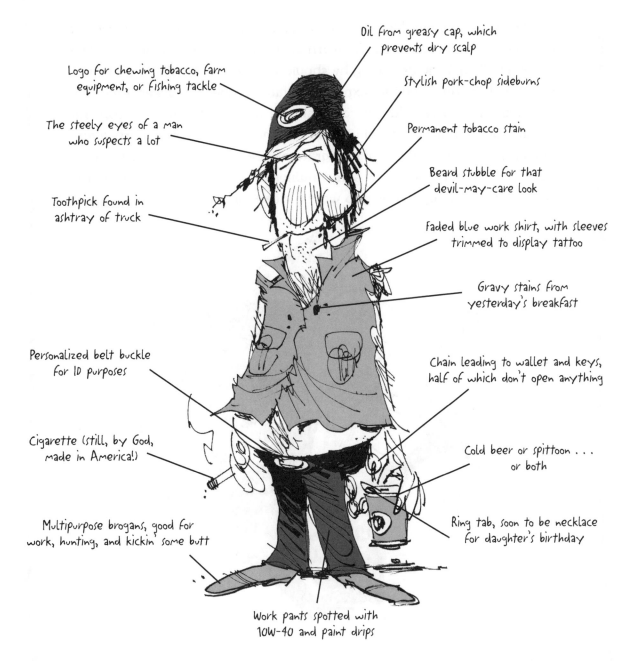

Oil from greasy cap, which prevents dry scalp

Logo for chewing tobacco, farm equipment, or fishing tackle

Stylish pork-chop sideburns

The steely eyes of a man who suspects a lot

Permanent tobacco stain

Beard stubble for that devil-may-care look

Toothpick found in ashtray of truck

Faded blue work shirt, with sleeves trimmed to display tattoo

Gravy stains from yesterday's breakfast

Personalized belt buckle for ID purposes

Chain leading to wallet and keys, half of which don't open anything

Cigarette (still, by God, made in America!)

Cold beer or spittoon . . . or both

Multipurpose brogans, good for work, hunting, and kickin' some butt

Ring tab, soon to be necklace for daughter's birthday

Work pants spotted with 10W-40 and paint drips

Hats

Hats fall into a definite hierarchy for rednecks. First and forever foremost is the baseball cap, which can be worn year-round. When a redneck gets a new baseball cap, the first thing he should do is bend the bill so it forms a perfect half-moon. Nothing exposes a faux redneck quicker than the unshaped bill of a cap. Ideally, caps should have logos on the crown for chewing tobacco, heavy machinery, an automobile, beer, or a sports team. They may be worn until they disintegrate or need an oil change, whichever comes first. I have heard of some rednecks washing their caps in the dishwasher, but if you're going to wear a clean hat, why not just get a new

one? Then you can put the old one on the dashboard of your truck, where it belongs. A true redneck never throws away a cap.

Second in the redneck hat hierarchy is the cowboy hat with the sides curled up. These hats are typically made of straw (perfect for pulling out the occasional toothpick) and may include a number of decorations, such as

- *Feathers:* Chicken feathers are fine as long as you avoid those from the tail section, for obvious reasons. Hawk feathers say "outdoorsman," eagle feathers say "felon," and peacock feathers say you could be a switch-hitter. Personally, I would avoid the peacock feathers.

- *Snake parts:* Snakeskin makes an impressive band around any hat. It also offers the opportunity to tell a whopper of a story about how you slew the serpent (most rednecks think molting is what happens when you leave the freezer door open). The best snake part of all is rattlers; if you choose to harvest these yourself, I recommend a very long-handled hoe and hip waders.

- *Ticket stubs:* As a colorful memento of special events—truck pulls, cockfights, pro wrestling matches, NASCAR races, and so on—some rednecks tuck their ticket stubs behind their hatbands. Avoid the temptation to include stubs from parking tickets.

Third in hat hierarchy is the bucket or fishing hat. These are readily identifiable by the various lures hanging from the hat. Removing the line before attaching the lures will give the hat a tidier appearance. Also remove any remaining bait before attaching the lures.

Jewelry

The only jewelry a redneck should ever wear is an arm clock, often referred to as a watch. It's best if the watch doesn't work, so you won't be bothered when you're late for work or an appointment. (*Note:* Real Rolexes don't turn green on your wrist and are seldom sold outside the 7-Eleven.)

Pants

Denim and cotton tend to be the fabrics of choice for pants. Denim can hold more grease and oil between washings, but cotton is easier to sew after the crotch rips out. If you can find the "expand-o-matic" waistbands that stretch up to four inches, I highly recommend them; you'd be surprised how much more you can eat while wearing those bad-boys.

Shirts

T-shirts, particularly the kind with a single front pocket for smokes, remain the leader among shirts. Either the front or the back should include the name and logo of a motorized vehicle, a band and its tour schedule, or a witty saying such as "I'm with Stupid ➤." Old baseball warm-up shirts and football jerseys are always popular and can even make the "favorite" list once they become faded and torn.

Knit shirts with collars (often called polo shirts by people who never saw a horse from the rear end, or golf shirts by those with club crests on their blazers) are comfortable when worn with the shirttail out. Be sure the front hem is about an inch short of covering your belly so it doesn't obstruct the view of your belt buckle.

Short-sleeve shirts are appropriate for evening wear as long as you don't button them all the way (two buttons is usually ideal). In cool weather, a T-shirt under an unbuttoned shirt is not only stylish but functional. In honest-to-God cold weather, like so cold your truck won't start, the first step is to layer flannel shirts—four layers is the usual limit. If that's not enough to toast your chestnuts, a work jacket with a frayed collar and cuffs should do the trick. An old high-school letter jacket is the absolute height of fashion, but remember that no redneck worth his saltines ever wore an overcoat.

You've worn boxer shorts as an outer garment.

You Might Be a Redneck If . . .

Your underwear is older than your wife.

☆

Your best shirt has someone else's name
embroidered above the pocket.

☆

You failed to meet the dress code
at the fairgrounds.

☆

Your best jacket advertises farm machinery.

☆

You ever bought a used cap.

☆

Your favorite shirt has 10 jokes on the back.

You Might Be a Redneck If . . .

You consider your softball uniform
"dressy casual."

Someone asks to see your ID
and you show them your belt buckle.

You wore a beer-dispensing cap
to your kid's Little League game.

You've ever left a pair of underwear
in the woods.

Your "Arizona State" T-shirt is
from the penitentiary, not the university.

You and your wife have the same measurements.

☆

People have grown weary of telling you
your pants are unzipped.

☆

It's impossible to see food stains on the fabric
of your work uniform.

The key to
your spring
wardrobe is
a pair of
scissors.

Care of Clothing

Sweat stains detract from the beauty of any shirt or jacket. Because the salt deposits from such stains are not suitable for table use anyway, I recommend having your nice clothes professionally cleaned and pressed. An iron that's too hot can spell disaster for even the best polyester.

You Might Be a Redneck If . . .

Your mailbox holds up one end of your clothesline.

People are scared to touch your bathrobe.

☆

You think money laundering is when
you accidentally wash bills in your pants pocket.

☆

People drive from miles away to look
at your grandma's underpants hanging
on the clothesline.

☆

You go to the Laundromat to pick up women.

☆

The cleaners inform you that they can't get
out the sweat stains.

☆

You're naked on laundry day.

HOW MANY WOMEN DOES IT TAKE TO CHANGE A REDNECK?

- NOBODY KNOWS—IT'S NEVER BEEN DONE.

- ONE DIVORCED TATTOO ARTIST WITH A BAD ATTITUDE.

- THREE—HIS MAMA HOLDING HIS TRUCK KEYS, HIS WIFE HOLDING A SHOTGUN, AND THE JUDGE HOLDING A GAVEL.

- JUST ONE—HIS EX-WIFE, COUSIN, AND SISTER-IN-LAW.

- FOUR—ONE TO HOLD HIS BEER, TWO TO UNDO HIS OVERALLS, AND ONE TO PULL ON A CLEAN PAIR OF UNDERDRAWERS.

- ONE, IF HER NAME IS HILLARY CLINTON. SHE EVEN PUT HER REDNECK IN THE WHITE HOUSE!

Dining

Redneck men have pretty simple tastes when it comes to food:

- We like meat with every meal. And contrary to what most wives believe, Vienna Sausages, potted meat, and pork skins are legitimate meats.

- We like our steaks rare but our bacon crisp.

- Barbecue is pork. We may argue about the sauces, but that much is indisputable.

- We usually save wild game to serve when fellow rednecks are eating with us, so we can share the exciting details of the hunt.

- We want bread at every meal. That means doughnuts for breakfast, saltines at lunch, and biscuits or cornbread with supper.

- We prefer everything fried in shortening or lard, not in vegetable oil. Everybody knows there ain't no oil in vegetables.

- Tomatoes should be sliced thick and served at room temperature. Those little cherry tomatoes should be left alone until they grow into full-size tomatoes.

- We don't like any vegetable that crunches when eaten.

- Last but not least, there is the ultimate redneck food that can be enjoyed anytime and anywhere—jerky. It's delicious even with the wrapper on.

There are times, however, when women insist on eating a meal someplace other than on a TV tray or in a car. As many dining establishments require shirts and shoes, such occasions may call for planning on your part. I recommend keeping a clean pair of jeans and a fresh T-shirt in the trunk of your car. When properly positioned, these can also serve to keep the jack from rattling.

Orderly Ordering

When dining out, it is not only acceptable for the man to order for his female companion, but a recommended method for controlling the economic outflow for the evening. Nothing can be more embarrassing for a man than having to counter his date's "I think I'll have the deluxe platter" with "Think again." And when left to make their own decisions, women will always want that pricey side order of French fries.

As a matter of pure convenience, it is easier for the man to order since he is usually driving and is closer to the speaker.

Getting the Waiter's Attention

For unknown reasons, waiters are seldom waiting when you need them. Therefore, you occasionally must take measures to get their attention. If the waiter is only a couple of tables away, a sharp whistle will usually do the trick. If he is across the room, however, nothing solicits a quicker response than throwing a biscuit at his head. (*Note:* Throw only fresh biscuits. A man in Illinois hit his target with a day-old number and was charged with aggravated assault.)

Ordering Wine

In fancy restaurants, wine bottles usually come sealed with a cork instead of a screw-on cap. Consider this a bonus and pocket the cork for a future fishing trip.

It is the responsibility of the person who orders the wine to taste it beforehand. (*Note*: Gargling is frowned upon.) If the wine is bad, do not spit it out and yell, "Somebody forgot to wash their feet before they stomped these grapes!" Just swallow it and make a sincere effort to keep it down.

When decanting wine, make sure that you tilt the paper cup and pour slowly so as not to "bruise" the fruit of the vine. If drinking directly from the bottle, always hold it with your fingers covering the label.

Table Conversation

Try to avoid any stories about car wrecks, operations, roadkill, or sick pets. Nothing ruins a good meal quicker than someone getting sick or sentimental at the table.

While perfectly okay at home, it is considered crass when dining out to ask, "Are you gonna eat the rest of that meatloaf?" This is especially true if you don't know the person.

Leftovers

At the end of a meal, it is perfectly okay to ask your waiter or waitress for a box so you can take scraps home to your dog. Remember, however, to remove the chicken bones and cold grits, as both can choke a dog in a heartbeat.

Many establishments frown on the use of a "doggie box" at the all-you-can-eat salad bar. Avoid such pretentious places.

You Might Be a Redneck If . . .

You carry Ziploc bags
in your pocket for leftovers.

☆

You've reheated a Big Mac
with your windshield defroster.

You've ever smuggled
food out of an
all-you-can-eat
buffet.

Dining Q&A

Q: Where should you leave your silverware
when you have finished eating?
A: Standing in your water glass.

Q: When is it proper to be seated?
A: After your hostess is seated, or whenever
you feel gas coming on.

Q: Is it okay to dip your bread in gravy?
A: Only if the gravy is on your own clothes.

Q: What is the correct way to pass food around the table?
A: Overhanded, especially if you can put
a nice spiral on a sweet potato.

☆

Q: Is it proper to reach across the table?
A: Yes, as long as you keep one foot on the floor,
just as in shooting pool.

Q: What is too big a bite?
A: If you've got one end in your teeth and the
other in your hand, and your hand is more than
six inches from your mouth, that's too big a bite.

You Might Be a Redneck If . . .

You think Starbucks is a hunting ranch.

☆

You've ever picked your teeth with a menu.

☆

Your favorite restaurant is 7-Eleven.

☆

You think caviar is an imported hatchback.

☆

Your favorite meal is available only at county fairs.

☆

You think American Express is a take-out diner.

☆

Your favorite restaurant is attached to a car wash.

You Might Be a Redneck If . . .

The most expensive meal you ever bought came
with a moist towelette.

You think Kung Pao Chicken
is a martial arts movie.

Your favorite meal has a combo number.

Your wife sleeps on the couch
every time you eat at Taco Bell.

You make your kids lie about their ages
to qualify for kids' meals.

You walk into a restaurant with a toothpick in your mouth.

You Might Be a Redneck If . . .

You think Lamborghini is a special
at the Olive Garden.

A fortune cookie changed your life.

You think *haute cuisine* is after it comes
out of the microwave.

You've ever stopped to use the bathroom
in a fast-food restaurant but didn't buy anything.

You think Condoleezza Rice
is an alternative to fried rice.

Your favorite restaurant also sells propane.

You hope heaven is kind of like Hooters.

☆

The owner of a restaurant had to ask you,
"Please move away from the salad bar
before you start eating."

☆

You had your anniversary dinner
at the food court in the mall.

☆

You think "dinner reservations" means
they've tasted your wife's cooking.

☆

You've ever ordered a bucket of skin from KFC.

Tips on Dining in Others' Homes

Rules for this experience fall about halfway between eating at home (no shirt, no problem) and dining out (no shirt, no service). In other words, you should wear a shirt but it doesn't have to be buttoned. Here are several other tips about eating at somebody else's house.

- Wipe your feet before entering so you don't bring in what they sent the dog outside to do.

- When eating at a friend's house, it is generally considered rude to ask what a particular dish is. Besides, you may discover that you really don't want to know all the ingredients in "Roadkill Casserole."

- A loud burp at the table can be embarrassing for everyone. After such an incident, it is the host or hostess's responsibility to put the group at ease by saying something like, "Sounds better since you had it tuned."

- Remember that not everyone thinks like you do. When visiting others, establish early in the evening what is okay and what is not okay to spit in.

- Don't put your feet on the table during dinner to show off your new half-soles.

Many times you will need a good weapon for breaking large joints or hacking away at fur or fat. If your host or hostess does not provide you with the proper instruments for your culinary experience, it is perfectly okay to remove your personal knife or hatchet from your belt and use it. Often a choice morsel hides just beneath an inch or so of gristle. Do not, however, bang the handle of your knife with a ketchup bottle; you could damage the blade.

When you have finished using the knife, it should be wiped clean on the tablecloth and returned to its sheath or stuck into the table. Remember, however, that Formica is very hard and can dull the tip of even the finest Buck knife.

You Might Be a Redneck If . . .

You've ever overdosed on Kool-Aid.

☆

You think lowering your carb intake
involves working on your truck.

☆

You inherited heartburn.

☆

Your favorite green vegetable is dill pickles.

☆

Healthy foods give you indigestion.

☆

You crave cotton candy.

☆

Your burps set off smoke detectors.

HOW MANY WOMEN DOES IT TAKE TO CHANGE A REDNECK?

FOR JESSICA SIMPSON, HE'LL CHANGE BY HIMSELF— FROM A GOOD OL' BOY TO A DROOLING FOOL.

Entertaining

As you climb the social and professional ladders, you may find yourself often entertaining guests. Here are tips to make sure their visit is a memorable one.

- Go the extra mile and take out the trash a couple of days before guests arrive. It is difficult to be witty when your nose burns from the odors of rotting kitchen scraps.

- Prepare your house for visitors. Nothing can bring conversation to a screeching halt quicker than the loud snap of a rattrap. If this social nightmare should occur, the host is not obliged to show the victim to the group . . . unless they ask to see it.

- A little imagination can make your home look its best. Cover those nasty burn holes in the carpet with strategically placed old newspapers or a basket of dirty clothes.

- If you have a clothesline in your front yard, it is in good taste to remove the clothes before receiving guests. The underwear can tell others more than they really want to know about you and your family.

- While a wise use of time, guests may feel snubbed if your wife continues to iron clothes while the group chats. There'll be plenty of time for her to finish that task after the guests leave and you go to bed.

- During flood season, refrain from entertaining until all the water has receded from the living room.

- Make your guests feel at home. Let them adjust the rabbit ears on the TV, and make the dog give up the couch.

- An alert host or hostess always provides an appetizer. A few cans of Vienna Sausages, a Spam loaf, and a box of Ritz crackers can really start an evening off on the right foot. Be careful when serving leftovers. A good rule of thumb is, "If the dogs won't eat it, company probably won't either."

- Even if a guest is extremely talkative and dominating the conversation, refrain from saying, "How 'bout putting some teeth in that hole."

- Always wipe your hands before picking your teeth.

- A centerpiece for the table should never be anything prepared by a taxidermist.

- Do not allow your dog to eat at the table . . . no matter how good his manners are.

- Be considerate of your guest. Point out in advance where the injury-threatening springs are located on the sofa.

- In summertime, be sure to provide each guest with his or her own flyswatter.

- If guests overstay their welcome, it may be necessary to give them hints that it's time to leave. I suggest a gentle reminder such as, "Y'all are either going to have to leave or chip in on the rent." If that doesn't work, call the law and report that you've got squatters.

- A host or hostess is expected to provide matches for the bathroom. I recommend spending the extra money for wooden matches; they are twice as effective as paper ones.

- A guest is not required to inform the group how many matches the performance demanded. Any damages resulting from explosions are the responsibility of the person who struck the match.

You Might Be a Redneck If . . .

Your favorite recipe begins, "Pierce the film covering."

☆

You've ever cooked with WD-40.

☆

Every time your wife makes dinner she says,
"It'll taste just like chicken."

You've ever carved
a turkey with a
chain saw.

You Might Be a Redneck If . . .

You think *hors d'oeuvres* are those girls
who hang out at the intersection downtown.

☆

Your toilet tissue is Taco Bell napkins.

☆

You keep a musical instrument in the bathroom.

☆

Your bathroom towels double
as your bathroom curtains.

☆

You think Rolex is bathroom tissue.

Conversation

Conversation is a necessary part of entertaining, particularly when the cable or dish is out of service. Although redneck men often project the image of the strong, silent type (when beer is not involved), there are certain subjects they enjoy talking about:

- NASCAR—anything from carburetor restrictor plates to whether Junior Johnson could have handled Dale Earnhardt when both were in their primes

- Pickup trucks—Ford vs. Chevy, on-demand 4WD vs. constant AWD, regular cab vs. king cab, spray-in liner vs. removable liner, hemi vs. turbo, and all options in between

- The proper way to boil peanuts

- Jessica Simpson, Pamela Anderson, and Paris Hilton

- Red Man vs. Beechnut

- Harley Sportster vs. Softail

- Fishing holes and deer stands

- Big-screen TVs and dish vs. cable

Likewise, there are a few subjects that rednecks absolutely do *not* want to discuss:

- Female problems

- Their wives' feelings

- Oprah Winfrey / Dr. Phil

- Thread counts

- Figure skating

- Ballroom dancing

- Makeup (not to be confused with make-up sex)

- Their kids' report cards

Unfortunately, not everyone is as enlightened as rednecks, and you may find that such people are not capable of discussing things that interest you. This can be extremely awkward, so I have come up with a few conversation starters. Here are a few lines proven effective in breaking the ice:

- How much you want for that refrigerator on the front porch?

- My old lady wants to get to know you.

- Let's step out on the porch where the flies ain't so bad.

- Is that an extra-firm mattress on top of your car?

- I bought some pearls just like those at a yard sale last weekend.

- Whose feet stink?

- Do I have anything stuck in my teeth?

- How long have you had that thing growing on your nose?

- Is that a new tattoo?

- When's your parole up?

- Dang, are those things real?

You have a limp that resulted
from a botched pick-up line.

☆

You've ever made animal noises
at a beauty pageant.

☆

You've broken wind
into a karaoke machine.

Rednecks Just Wanna Have Fun

It ain't easy being red. The average redneck has to work almost as many days as he hunts and fishes, provide a nice trailer for his wife and yard rats, keep at least one of the six cars and trucks in his yard running, tell the President and Congress what they ought to be doing, and remember jokes until he sees his buddies again.

With such a daily burden to bear, it's no wonder that when a redneck gets a chance to kick back and relax, he does it full bore. Here are a few ways to tell if you're a redneck just having a little fun:

- You set off fireworks at least once a week.
- You've tried to call a 1-900 number collect.
- You moved into a doublewide to accommodate your wide-screen TV.
- You raided your savings account—your truck's ashtray.
- You've ignited a bodily emission.
- You've ever buried a firearm.
- You can recite the alcohol content of all major beer brands.
- The only book in your home is propping up the sofa.
- You've ever been ejected from the bleachers at a Little League game.
- You think Beverly Hills is a topless dancer.
- You can't remember a single New Year's Eve.
- You've ever been restrained by bailiffs in small claims court.

- The Fire Marshal bans you from barbecuing.
- You declared bankruptcy to avoid video store late charges.
- The most comfortable seat in your house is the commode.
- You've ever been read your Miranda rights by an animal control officer.
- Neighbors come to see you for tire-swing advice.
- You've ever belched while saying, "I love you."
- You've ever been too drunk to fish.

- You keep an emergency pack of Marlboros duct-taped under your dashboard.
- You've ever voted for your cousin in a wet T-shirt contest.
- You keep a bottle opener in the shower.
- You've ever exited a courthouse with your shirt pulled over your head.
- You've sprinted across a baseball field . . . naked.
- You spent more than two nights in a row on other people's sofas.
- When you were interviewed about the tornado, you had to be "bleeped."
- You've smuggled cigarettes into a hospital.
- You've entered an insanity plea in traffic court.
- You've ever used a backscratcher down your pants.
- Everyone gets out of the public pool when you get in.
- You've ever shooed animals out of your yard with bottle rockets.

- Everyone who visits your home asks when it will be finished.
- You've ever crossed a state line on an inner tube.

- Your last vacation ended with a relative wiring you money.
- You've jumped through a restroom window to escape a bar tab.
- You get carpal tunnel syndrome from the TV remote.
- You've ever mooned a security camera.
- You've read an entire *Auto Trader* in one visit to the bathroom.
- Police dust your furniture more often than you do.
- You pioneered "drive-by hunting."
- The chairs in your living room are stackable.
- You've never stayed at a motel without stealing something.
- You've ever participated in a burp-off.
- Your idea of lawn maintenance is a can of gasoline and a lighter.
- Your best hunting dog has three legs.
- You've ever used a Slurpee as a cocktail mixer.
- Your favorite CD is available only at truck stops.
- Two of your kids were the result of a drunken misunderstanding.
- Your daddy lives in a gated community—prison.
- The emergency room doctor has ever said to you, "See you next weekend."
- You've ever tried to go down your porch steps on a pogo stick.
- You've ever watched an entire movie at an electronics store.
- You've ever released a hostage in exchange for a pizza.
- The grocery store manager asked you to stop harassing the lobsters.
- The last time you ran a mile, you were being chased.

HOW MANY WOMEN DOES IT TAKE TO CHANGE A REDNECK?

ONLY ONE, IF SHE CAN BAIT A HOOK, FIELD DRESS A DEER, DANCE AROUND A POLE, AND REBUILD A CARBURETOR.

Dating
(Outside the Family)

A good bloodline deserves to be protected, so I say don't date or marry outside the family unless it's absolutely necessary. But if all your cousins are taken and you're forced to look outside, here is some advice:

- Asking a woman for a date can be a nerve-wracking experience, because all men fear rejection. But just remember—if she doesn't say no to anyone else, she probably won't say no to you. A typical intro might be, "Hello, Sybil. This is Jimbo Crosswater. Your brother shot my brother, remember? Well, if you aren't busy Friday night, do you want to go out to the farm and watch the cows mate?"

- Be aggressive. Let her know you're interested: "I've been wanting to go out with you since I read that stuff on the men's bathroom wall two years ago."

- Shower her with compliments: "You ain't near as ugly as your sister. And that scar barely shows when you get up close." Such praise will make her heart melt like margarine.

- One should always go to the door to pick up a date. An exception to this rule can be made if her family owns a dog that is currently involved in a civil suit, and the gentleman caller is unsure about how long or strong the dog's chain is.

- Establish with your date's parents what time she is expected back. Some fathers might say, "Ten o'clock." Others might say, "Monday." If the answer is the latter, it is your responsibility to get the girl to school on time.

- Be a gentleman: Always light your date's cigarette, cigar, or pipe.

- Spend your date dollars wisely. If a girl's name does not appear regularly on a water tower or an overpass, odds are good that the date will end in disappointment.

- Be considerate of your dating partner. Do not tell others the details of your intimate moments until after the date is concluded.

- Even if you can't get a date, avoid kidnapping. It's bad for your reputation.

- Although drinking beer, watching TV, and hanging around outside the liquor store are usually considered family activities, they also can be the basis of a good, economical date . . . especially if your date doesn't drink.

YALL...THIS HERE IS DEE DEE...

Movie Etiquette

Unless you got their name and phone number off a bathroom wall, most girls won't go to a drive-in movie until after you've taken them to a walk-in movie. Consider this an investment in your future.

In most cases you'll have to pick up the girl at her trailer, drive her to the movie, stand around out front while she waits to be seen by friends, buy her ticket, and buy her snacks. Yes, I know that seems unfair, but nobody ever said life was easy for a redneck.

Here are several other tips for walk-in movies:

- Do not ask the concession stand attendant for the nacho cheese recipe.

- Do not eat popcorn or candy left by earlier movie-goers.

- Refrain from talking to characters on the screen. Tests have proven that they can't hear you.

- Do not put your feet on the back of the seat in front of you without first removing your shoes and socks.

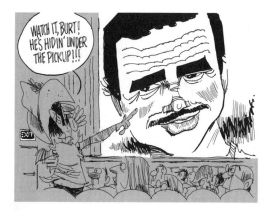

- If your date brings her baby along and it starts crying during the movie, the baby should be taken to the lobby and picked up immediately after the movie has ended.

You Might Be a Redneck If . . .

The last time you took your girlfriend
to the movies, she had to hide in the trunk.

☆

You honk your horn during love scenes at the drive-in.

☆

The first drive-in movie you saw
was from across the road.

You've ever
spray-painted
your
girlfriend's
name on an
overpass.

Inside the Redneck Heart

Some women think redneck men are callous and uncaring because they never cry over sappy movies or the death of a mother-in-law. But the truth is that redneck men are incredibly sensitive about certain subjects:

Dogs: Few things will bring a redneck man to tears quicker than the death of a good dog. The two have usually hunted together, scratched together, lain on the sofa together, and slept in the same doghouse on occasion. And no dog ever ratted when a redneck's wife demanded, "Where the hell have you been all night?" The loss of such a loyal friend will expose the tenderest side of a redneck.

Trucks: As long as a redneck man has his truck, he's always got a place to sleep, eat, and get out of the rain. He is the master of that domain, where he never has to pick up after himself, can leave cigarette butts in the ashtray, can listen to Willie and Waylon until the grooves are burned off the CD, and can keep the temperature as cold or hot as he pleases. It doesn't get any better than that.

Mamas: Bless their snuff-dipping, pea-shelling, biscuit-making, wig-wearing souls! These paragons of goodness tried to teach their sons the difference between right and wrong . . . and then whupped the dickens out of us when we made the wrong choice. But woe be unto anyone who puts down a redneck's mama or questions her sanctity.

You Might Be a Redneck If . . .

You've ever flirted
over a drive-thru window speaker.

☆

A dating service matches you up with a relative.

☆

You've ever French-kissed
within five feet of a Dumpster.

☆

You dated your daddy's current wife
in high school.

☆

You ask a girl to dance and she takes off her
clothes and climbs on a table.

☆

You consider dating second cousins
to be "playing the field."

You Might Be a Redneck If . . .

Your mother genuinely admires
your girlfriend's tattoos.

You Might Be a Redneck If . . .

You refer to your van as "the Love Machine."

A woman says she's game, so you shoot her.

☆

You view the upcoming family reunion
as a chance to meet women.

☆

You think "showing a girl a good time"
means letting her bait the hook.

☆

You've had more court dates than second dates.

When people talk about the Big Easy, you think they are referring to your ex-girlfriend.

You Might Be a Redneck If . . .

Your definition of "getting lucky"
is passing the emissions test.

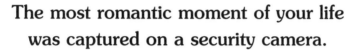

The most romantic moment of your life
was captured on a security camera.

★

You whistle at women in church.

★

You've ever used food stamps on a date.

★

All of your cousins are "kissing cousins."

★

You select a date's corsage to match her tattoo.

You've ever slow danced at a
Waffle House.

HOW MANY WOMEN DOES IT TAKE TO CHANGE A REDNECK?

DEPENDS ON HOW BIG HIS DIAPERS ARE.

Weddings

If you take a girl on a date and forget to take her home, it may be time to think about the next step—holy matrimony, joyful union, wedded bliss. Some people use those phrases to describe marriage, but rednecks often use more colorful phrases, such as hitched, ball and chain, and ring in the nose. But regardless of what you call it, the process is complicated and, if not handled well, can lead to bruised feelings and other parts. That's why I've gone to great trouble to explain the whole wedding process. You can thank me later.

Announcement

It is the responsibility of the bride's family to announce the wedding in the local newspaper. The announcement should include a photograph of the bride (a high school yearbook picture is acceptable), the name of the groom and his parents (if known), education completed by both the bride and groom (do not include elementary school, unless that was the terminal degree), current employment (if applicable), and planned residence after the ceremony (if living with the bride's parents, it is not necessary to specify in which room the couple will reside).

Invitations

For planned weddings (at least nine months prior to a blessed event), any couple expecting to get a lot of free stuff must send out invitations. They do not have to be lengthy. Something like, "You are invited to watch Scooter and Tracie make it legal on March 5," will suffice nicely.

Invitations to short-notice weddings (less than nine months prior to a blessed event) may be delivered orally in a bar or on the work site by saying, "If you ain't doing nothin' Saturday, why don't you stop by for a cold one 'bout two o'clock. Me and Tracie's having some friends over to watch the ball game and witness our wedding."

Proper Attire

For the bride, the key phrase is, "Be conservative." No matter how good it may look, your bride should refrain from wearing outfits made with Spandex or adorned with fringe. Excessive slits and dips also are frowned upon. This is not the day to show the world how big "they" really are.

Here's another valuable hint: a bridal veil made of window screen is not only cost effective but also is a proven fly deterrent.

For the groom, a rented tuxedo is *haute couture,* but if the cost means the difference between going on a honeymoon and staying home, consider some alternatives. For example, a leisure suit with a cummerbund and a clean bowling shirt can create an elegant appearance. Though they can be uncomfortable, say yes to socks and shoes for this special occasion.

The Ceremony

No matter how urgent the event, loaded weapons have no place at the altar. And at the point in the ceremony where the preacher says, "If anybody has any reason why these two should not be joined in holy matrimony . . . ," he is advised not to pause too long. Old flames sometimes die hard and talk too much.

As the ceremony is concluded, the bride and groom are reminded that a short kiss will do. This is neither the time nor place to demonstrate their sexual expertise to the world. That's why they make VCRs.

Reception Tips

- Remember to reserve the VFW far in advance, and avoid Saturdays because that's square dancing night.

- It is perfectly acceptable to ask guests to wipe their feet before entering the hall. After all, the cleaning deposit can be the difference between an oil change and a full tune-up for the pickup.

- When going through the receiving line, it is proper to say something nice to the bride, such as, "Your baby is real cute."

- Stealing liquor from an open bar is a no-no.

- If someone asks where the bride is registered, do not answer, "The American Kennel Club."

- Livestock usually is a poor choice for a wedding gift.

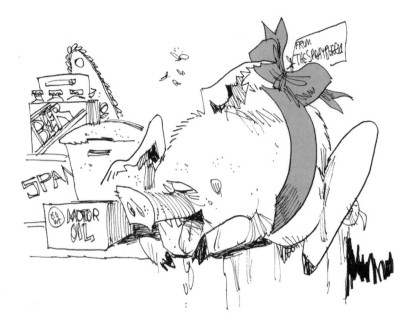

- Kissing the bride for more than five seconds may get you cut.

- Never ask someone to be in your wedding if attending would violate that person's parole.

- When dancing, do not remove undergarments, no matter how hot it is.

- When throwing rice at the bride and groom, use uncooked rice and toss it underhand.

- Never pocket the rice instead of throwing it, no matter how tough times are.

- If the wedding is canceled, the girl should return the ring. If her brother has already killed the groom-to-be, the ring should be returned to his next of kin.

Common Wedding Questions

Q: Is it all right to bring a date to a wedding?
A: Not if you are the groom.

Q: How many showers is the bride
supposed to have?
A: At least one the week of the wedding.

Q: How many bridal attendants
should the bride have?
A: One for each of her kids.

Q: What music is recommended
for the wedding ceremony?
A: Anything except "Tied to the Whipping Post."

You Might Be a Redneck If . . .

Your wedding limo had antlers on the hood.

☆

You leave space in your wedding album for "Next Time."

☆

You signed your marriage license
on the hood of a car.

☆

Your wedding photographer
used a disposable camera.

☆

You requested the honeymoon suite at Motel 6.

☆

Your wedding cake was made
of Twinkies and Cool Whip.

You Might Be a Redneck If . . .

At your wedding reception, you added Alka-Seltzer to cheap wine to make "champagne."

☆

Your current wife was a bridesmaid at your first wedding.

There were dogs in church on your wedding day.

You Might Be a Redneck If . . .

Your wedding day began in a liquor store
and ended in a tattoo parlor.

The stripper at your bachelor
party was your fiancée.

Two of your wedding videos made
America's Funniest Home Videos.

All your wedding photos have someone
torn out of them.

Your proposal to your wife started
with the words, "When I get out . . ."

You spent your wedding night on a La-Z-Boy.

You Might Be a Redneck If . . .

Your bride's wedding dress was
an animal print.

You Might Be a Redneck If . . .

Your prenuptial agreement mentioned chickens.

☆

At least one dog slept in your bed
on your wedding night.

☆

You've been told, "Repeat after me,"
by a preacher and a court officer on the same day.

☆

You used your daughter's wedding
as an excuse to buy a new shotgun.

☆

Your wedding ring was in a pawnshop on your
wedding morning and back there by closing time.

☆

You've had three weddings but no anniversaries.

You Might Be a Redneck If . . .

You bought a marriage license
and a fishing license on the same day.

☆

You received a jar of pickled eggs as a wedding gift.

The most expensive part of your wedding was your bride's tattoo removal.

You Might Be a Redneck If . . .

You won your wife's engagement ring by
knocking down three milk bottles with a baseball.

☆

You've given an oil change as a wedding gift.

☆

You've ever told a bride,
"You clean up pretty good."

☆

You honeymooned in the pop-up camper
in your parents' backyard.

☆

You have a picture of your bride,
in her wedding dress, holding a string of fish.

☆

You've been married three times
and still have the same in-laws.

You taped WWF wrestling
over your wedding video.

☆

You refer to the church where you were married
as "the scene of the crime."

You delayed
your
wedding
because of
hunting
season.

HOW MANY WOMEN DOES IT TAKE TO CHANGE A REDNECK?

○ ONE GOOD SOUTHERN WOMAN WOULD HAVE HIM TOILET TRAINED IN A NEW YORK MINUTE!

○ DEPENDS ON HOW SHE LOOKS, HOW MUCH SHE WEIGHS, AND IF HER FAMILY HAS ANY PROPERTY TO HUNT ON.

○ A TON, AND HER NAME IS SALLY AND SHE IS ALWAYS HOLDING A FRYING PAN.

○ ONE WHO OWNS A 1977 *SMOKEY AND THE BANDIT* TRANS-AM WITH A 400 CI, 6.6 LITER ENGINE, AND A FOUR-SPEED WITH A HURST SHIFTER.

○ JUST ONE: LORENA BOBBITT.

Fatherhood

The only thing as strong as the bond between a redneck father and his son is the bond between a redneck father and his daughter.

Sons

With a son, you get to pass on all the lessons, tricks, and traits that you've picked up along the way, such as:

- How to undo a bra without spilling your beer

- How to tuck a cigarette behind your ear

- How to move a sofa on a skateboard

- Your "system" for winning the lottery

- How to light charcoal without singeing your eyebrows

- How to sight a rifle on the birdbath

- How to urinate "I Luv U" in the snow

- How to make a fake ID

- A dozen different uses for old tires

- How to trim a shrub into the shape of a naked woman

- Five uses for a baseball bat, other than hitting balls

- How to avoid rug burns

- How to train for eating contests

- How to pan for gold with a colander

- How to open a beer can with your toes

- How to bandage a wound with duct tape

- How to open a can of chili with a handgun

- How to make a Jet Ski out of a motorcycle

Daughters

With a daughter, you get to teach her all the things you wish your wife knew, such as:

- Cellulite is not a mobile phone company

- How to dry clothes in the microwave

- Never wear a muumuu to a job interview

- How to park an 18-wheeler

- Granola is not your mom's mom

- How to find "markdowns" at the Dollar Store

- Switching to light beer is not going on a diet

- Don't fake a pregnancy to get shower gifts

- Wedding rings are not supposed to change colors

- It is possible to go to Vegas and not come home pregnant

- Hiding hickeys is not a job skill

- Don't wear lingerie to see the gynecologist

- Not everything at a yard sale is worth fighting over

- Jell-O is not one of the major food groups

- A storage unit is not "a second home"

- Don't plan your wedding during hunting season

- Don't tell anyone about your conversations with Elvis

- Don't use a Sharpie as eyeliner

The Teenage Years

With both sons and daughters, the teenage years usually are the hardest on parents.

Everything a son does from the age of about 12 to about 80 is influenced by testosterone, which is sort of like octane in gasoline. The higher the octane, the hotter it burns, and it's highest during the teenage years. In sports, his main motivator for winning will be to impress girls. In school, he'll intentionally fail so he can get access to another grade level of girls. He'll even pretend to be interested in macrame if it'll get him closer to a hot girl.

Teenage daughters also experience an increase in octane, but theirs is called estrogen. As the hormones increase, daughters become extremely interested in makeup, credit cards, clothes, and shoes. If they see a boy swimming naked in a creek, the first thing that pops into their minds is, "I bet he would look good in a flowered chintz." The hormones also contribute to their Jekyll and Hyde personalities for several days each month; if you're married, you know what I mean.

The main thing to remember about raising children is that they're usually the ones who will decide how you'll spend your final years. So unless you enjoy living in a cardboard box, don't be too hard on them.

You Might Be a Redneck If . . .

You cried the day your son tapped his first keg.

☆

You've ever changed a diaper on a Denny's table.

☆

Any of your children were conceived in a bass boat.

☆

You got your picture taken on Santa's knee,
but your kids didn't.

☆

You know how to fit three baby seats
in the back of a Trans Am.

☆

Your children's night-light is a neon beer sign.

Your kids take rabbit sandwiches
to school in their lunch boxes.

☆

You wore a giant foam finger
at your child's graduation.

The doctor
who delivered
your children
also delivers
your propane.

You Might Be a Redneck If . . .

Your children catch
frogs and lizards—inside the house.

☆

There are more kids than groceries
in your shopping cart.

☆

Your kids attended your high school graduation.

☆

Your mother taught you how to flip a cigarette.

☆

Your brothers are convinced
that you were an only child.

☆

Your kid was born with a plastic spoon in his mouth.

You Might Be a Redneck If . . .

Your kids take roadkill to show-and-tell.

Your kid ever told a caller, "Daddy will be back in three to five years."

You turn on your sprinkler and tell the kids it's a water park.

Your bumper sticker says, "My child whipped your honor student's ass."

☆

When describing your kids, you use the phrase "dumb as a brick."

☆

Your son's birth announcement ran in *Auto Trader*.

☆

Your kids steal the towels when they stay overnight with relatives.

You Might Be a Redneck If . . .

Your kids know your CB handle
but not your real name.

117

You Might Be a Redneck If . . .

There are big rigs named after your daughter.

☆

You've ever hollered, "You kids quit playing
on that sheet metal!"

☆

Your 14-year-old smokes in front of her kids.

☆

You bought a *Girls Gone Wild* video
because your daughter was in it.

☆

Your dogs mind better than your kids do.

☆

You punish your children
by taking away their chewing tobacco.

HOW MANY WOMEN DOES IT TAKE TO CHANGE A REDNECK?

ONE FEMALE JUDGE, AND THEN ONLY FOR THREE TO FIVE YEARS.

Behind the Wheel

Shortly after rednecks are potty trained, they begin learning to drive. And as soon as they have mastered starting and stopping, they begin customizing their cars and trucks. Stock is for cattle; rednecks want lots of chrome, big wheels, elaborate pinstripes, custom tags, and a stereo with enough watts to loosen a filling.

Favorite Vehicles

Although anything with a motor is desirable to a redneck on a bicycle, there are certain cars that historically have been associated with rednecks. First, of course, is the pickup truck.

You start with a basic used Ford, Chevy, Dodge, or GMC (according to a recent study, fewer than 10 percent of rednecks have ever owned a new truck). Then you add slip-on seat covers, a decal on the back window, a gun rack, a long, whippy antenna, three or four bumper stickers, and oversized mud tires that sing when you drive down the road. That rig will say "I'm a redneck" quicker than John Daly.

The Chevy Camaro and Pontiac Trans Am have long been favorites of rednecks. Both cars look like they're going fast even when they're sitting still, as redneck cars often are. Common touches on Camaros and Trans Ams include fuzzy dice, Mardi Gras beads, and/or graduation tassels hanging from the rearview mirror, chrome extensions on the tailpipes, a bent coat hanger for an antenna, mismatched tires, and doors that rattle like a bucket of bolts when they close.

More mature rednecks, who have made their marks in the world, often opt for used Cadillacs or Lincolns. These land yachts should have at least one window that won't go up, some part of the bumper missing, a piece of side-body trim hanging loose, a bent antenna, and no hood ornament. These cars make quite a statement, especially with a hole in the muffler.

Rules of the Road

Regardless of your ride, once you take to the road you should observe basic redneck rules. There are a number of road signs designed to help drivers be nice, such as Yield, Slow, and—my personal favorite—Take Gap, Give Gap. And contrary to popular belief, the sign telling you to "Merge" is not a challenge. When signs are not available, follow these tips for civil driving:

- Dim your headlights for approaching vehicles, even if the gun is loaded and the deer is in sight.

- Replace missing car doors as a courtesy to your passengers.

- When approaching a four-way stop, remember that the vehicle with the largest tires always has the right-of-way.

- Never tow another car using pantyhose and duct tape.

- Never play Chinese fire drill with handicapped passengers, especially if parked on a hill.

- When sending your wife down the road with a gas can, it is impolite to ask her to bring back beer.

- Never relieve yourself from a moving vehicle, especially when driving.

- When traveling with a mattress on top of the car, do not allow others to take a nap on it.

- Never fish from a moving vehicle.

- Do not remove the seats from a car so that all of your kids can fit in.

- Never make catcalls at women in another car if a big guy is traveling with them.

- When traveling with your family, try to keep their "mooning" of other drivers to a minimum.

- Remember that the median is not a passing lane.

- Don't spit tobacco out the window if you know the people following you.

- Do not lay rubber while traveling in a funeral procession.

- When towing a boat, insist that your fishing buddies ride inside the car.

- Never hit mailboxes with a baseball bat from a moving car, especially in your own neighborhood. Someone might recognize you.

You've washed an entire truck with baby wipes.

☆

Auto salvage yards consider you the competition.

You've ever broken the speed limit in reverse.

You Might Be a Redneck If . . .

You've ever touched up your truck's paint
with a Sharpie.

☆

Your boots have more tread than your tires.

☆

You say you're a student because
you're always at driving school.

☆

The model year of your car is 1974, 1976, and 1979.

☆

You still own every tire you ever bought.

☆

You hold the hood of your car open
with your head while you work on it.

Every car you own is for sale.

☆

Your truck has more lights than your house.

You slam the door on your truck and your shotgun creates an instant sunroof.

You Might Be a Redneck If . . .

You have to sign a release at the car wash.

☆

You painted your truck camouflage
and now you can't find it.

☆

The only Spanish you know is "El Camino."

☆

You wait in the car while your wife
changes a flat.

☆

You have a dozen license plates on your wall
but not one on your truck.

☆

Every time you slam on the brakes,
two dogs hit the dashboard.

You own eight cars but still have
to bum a ride to work.

The seat covers in your car are old T-shirts.

Locking your truck involves a padlock and chains.

Your car gets rear-ended and you can't tell.

You work on your car even when
there's nothing wrong with it.

You Might Be a Redneck If . . .

You've ever paid for a car with change.

☆

You own half of a pickup truck.

☆

You have a set of "monster mudder"
tires on your station wagon.

☆

You've ever used a bungee cord as a seat belt.

☆

You hand painted whitewalls on your tires.

☆

One of your car windows is a Hefty bag.

You taught your wife to drive so you would have a way home after parties.

Your car has a Papa John's sign on top.

You have a time-share on a Trans Am.

☆

You've ever driven 10 miles with a relative
on the roof rack.

☆

Your car's antitheft device
is the way it looks.

☆

Your mud flaps are illegal in 23 states.

☆

You've ever emptied the bed of your truck
by driving backwards real fast
and slamming on the brakes.

HOW MANY WOMEN DOES IT TAKE TO CHANGE A REDNECK?

○ JUST ONE WHOSE FAVORITE SPICE IS D-CON.

○ ONE—HIS FEMALE PHARMACIST TELLING HIM, "THAT SNUFF WILL MAKE YOU IMPOTENT."

ONLY ONE, IF SHE'S WEARING A RUBBER GLOVE.

Special Situations

In this book, I've tried to provide information about the most common situations where somebody might want to change a redneck or his behavior. Even so, there are special situations that don't come up very often but still deserve a word or two.

Hospital Etiquette

Rednecks generally try to avoid hospitals. For one thing, the food in hospitals is usually flavorless; why can't they use a little lard in the biscuits and bacon drippings in the vegetables? And no matter what your doctor says, liver is not good for you.

Another reason rednecks shy away from hospitals is those half-gowns, where your rear end shows when you walk down the hall. Rednecks don't mind showing their butts, but they prefer to do it in public and with the aid of drinking alcohol, not alcohol wipes.

Hospitals also charge a lot for supplies but won't let you bring your own. While an old T-shirt torn into strips makes a perfectly good dressing for wounds, most hospitals insist they're not sanitary, even if you washed the T-shirt before you wore it the last time.

133

Sooner or later, though, you'll probably have to visit a relative or friend in the hospital. I have discovered that most hospitalizations of rednecks are usually the result of someone saying, "Hey, y'all, watch this!" Chain saws and go-carts also are frequent causes.

When receiving visitors in the hospital, the patient is not expected to show strangers his incision. The same is true of elective surgery—not everyone is fascinated by a vasectomy.

When visiting friends in the hospital, one should always bring his or her own beer and fried chicken. While it is perfectly acceptable to fill an infirm friend's IV bag with a cold pop, one should never use a bedpan as a punch bowl or a plate.

Funeral Etiquette

If things don't go well in the hospital, the next time you see a friend could be at the funeral home. As sad as such occasions may be, rednecks generally try to focus on happier times. It is entirely appropriate for friends to gather around the deceased and tell stories, although it is recommended that discretion be used if the widow is in attendance. This is not the time for her to learn about previous indiscretions.

This is also not a good time to talk about the flesh-eating worms you heard about on TV. Or about the caskets that floated away the last time the river flooded. Or about grave robbers. Focus instead on stories about good deeds the deceased performed, like when he was asked to leave the high school

basketball game for disorderly conduct and did so without having to be escorted out.

The following are a few more tips for proper conduct when a redneck passes over:

Never postpone a burial by placing your loved one in the freezer "until money's not quite so tight."

If you are asked to deliver a eulogy, remember that you're supposed to honor the deceased. That does not mean, however, that you brag about his sexual exploits, his ability to hold his liquor, or the time he wrote poetry on the side of the gymnasium with spray paint.

It is considered improper to bury people on your own property—or anyone else's property—without their permission. In either case, the authorities frown on it.

When viewing the body, never say, "He looks so natural. Like he just got drunk and passed out."

And finally, even if you're certain that you are included in the will, it is considered inappropriate to drive a U-Haul to the funeral home.

You showed pictures of your latest deer
at the funeral home.

Your station wagon used to be a hearse.

You've ever asked a widow for
her phone number at the
funeral home.

136

Jailhouse and Courtroom Etiquette

On occasion, you may be called upon to visit the local lockup and subsequently appear before the magistrate. These things happen. And often as not, the consumption of alcoholic beverages is associated with such visits. Go figure.

When you are first invited to sit in the backseat of a squad car, do not ask the arresting officers to change the radio station. Also do not ask them to stop at the drive-thru window of your favorite burger joint. And certainly don't ask them to call your buddies and tell them you'll be a little late for the party.

At the station, turn over all your valuables to the desk clerk, including your key ring, belt buckle, and bottle opener. When she asks if you have anything else on your possession, do not say, "Frisk me," because it'll be the 300-pound patrolman who does the frisking, not the cute desk clerk.

After a day or two in jail, because nobody in your family can afford bond, you'll be taken before the judge. Whatever you do, don't ask, "Are you wearing anything under that robe?" It could be the last question you ask for the next 30 days.

You Might Be a Redneck If . . .

Tear gas was ever fired into your home.

☆

More than one person at your class reunion
was on a weekend pass for good behavior.

☆

You have a family portrait drawn
by a courtroom artist.

☆

The only time you ever moved was under
a witness protection program.

☆

You've ever appeared on TV
with your face digitally blurred.

You Might Be a Redneck If . . .

You consider your license plate personalized
because your father made it.

The last time you test-drove a car,
it ended in a police chase.

You turned in a family member
for the reward.

You've ever left a bingo game in handcuffs.

☆

You've practiced saying the words "not guilty."

The only words you say in court are, "I dunno."

☆

You've ever introduced someone as
"my court-appointed lawyer."

☆

You're driving the car being described
on the police scanner.

☆

Your attorney begs you not to take the stand.

☆

You've ever thrown up in a squad car.

☆

You've ever worn a wire to a family reunion.

The sheriff regularly speaks
to you through a megaphone.

You Might Be a Redneck If . . .

You can't schedule a family reunion until
after the parole board meets.

☆

You hear a siren and your first instinct is to hide.

☆

Police ever escorted you to the city limits.

☆

You got a speeding ticket
while towing another vehicle.

☆

Your high-school class voted you
"Most likely to return fire."

☆

You have more previous convictions
than previous employers.

You Might Be a Redneck If . . .

STIFFSOCK COUNTY SHERIFF DEPT.
OA 649-442-9884
JULY 3, 1989

STIFFSOCK COUNTY SHERIFF DEPT.
OA 649-442-9884
JULY 3, 1989

The last photos of your mother were taken from the front and the side.

The best photo of you
has a height chart as a backdrop.

☆

You can name more state penitentiaries
than state capitals.

Your cell number has nothing
to do with a telephone.

☆

Any of your children are the result of a conjugal visit.

You've ever surrendered to police in exchange for cigarettes.

YA'LL GOT ANYTHING TO SMOKE?

Tips For All Other Occasions

- Never allow a woman to walk through a mud puddle. That'll ruin a set of custom floor mats quicker than French fries.

- If a lady drops her handkerchief, always pick it up for her. If it has been used recently, use a stick.

- Don't make company sleep on dirty sheets. Provide them with directions to the nearest Laundromat.

- Rugs need to be occasionally beaten, not just threatened.

- Never set off a flea bomb in someone else's home without asking permission first.

- When your wife is giving birth, have a relative call her school so she won't be charged with an unexcused absence.

- Never go up to a stranger on the beach and ask if you can get that pimple on his back.

- Teach your children not to eat French fries found in other people's cars.

- It is considered tacky to take a cooler into church. Tailgating in the parking lot after church, however, is permitted.

- No matter how broke you are, never take your date flowers that were stolen from a cemetery.

- If your dog falls in love with a guest's leg, have the decency to leave them alone for a few minutes.

- Always identify people in your yard before shooting at them.

- Teach your children proper telephone etiquette. Nothing can be more embarrassing than when Junior says, "We ain't seen Daddy in eight days, and Mama's too drunk to come to the phone."

- Never ask someone else to hold your chew.

- Always say, "Excuse me," after getting sick in someone else's car.

- Open and close doors quietly—if you have them.

- When leaving town for the weekend, parents should not board their children at the local kennel.

- Never take a beer to a job interview.

- The socially refined never fish coins out of public fountains, especially if other people are watching.

- Prank phone calls should cease after the age of 30.

- If you have to vacuum the bed, it's time to change the sheets.

- When in public places, use public restrooms instead of the parking lot, potted plants, and balconies.

- Tip a valet if he has to push or jump-start your car.

- Always make sure that family members are prepared to provide an alibi for you.

HOW MANY WOMEN DOES IT TAKE TO CHANGE A REDNECK?

○ ONLY ONE, AS LONG AS SHE HAS A GOOD DIVORCE LAWYER.

○ NONE. WHY IN THE WORLD WOULD ANYONE EVER WANT TO CHANGE A REDNECK?

JUST ONE—
A BABY
GIRL.